Great Smoky Mountains National Park:

In the Beginning…Fact, Legend & Eminent Domain

Dr. Gail Palmer

"Dr. Gail Palmer has produced a large body of work on the Great Smoky Mountains that includes two books and two DVDs. Her most recent book, "Smoky Mountain Tales, Volume I: Feuds, Murder & Mayhem," shares a native's look at the mountain people, a captivating and entertaining model for communicating local history through storytelling."

East Tennessee Historical Society
2013 Community History Award

Cover photo: President Franklin D. Roosevelt, Courtesy, National Park Service; Cover photo: Smoky Mountains, Courtesy, Kathleen Puckett, Townsend, TN; Cover artwork: Linda Weaver, Alcoa, TN

President Franklin D. Roosevelt on Sept. 2, 1940, as he dedicates the Great Smoky Mountains National Park at Newfound Gap with one foot in North Carolina and one foot in Tennessee. Others on the platform include his wife, Eleanor, and Anne M. and Willis P. Davis. Photographer Paul A. Moore was the first photographer hired by Tennessee Dept. of Conservation in 1937. Much of his work is part of the photographic collections of the Tennessee State Archives.

.

This creative non-fiction book is based on talks, presentations and DVDs by Dr. Gail Palmer: *Sacred Places of the Smokies*, DVD; *When Mama Was the Doctor: Mountain Medicine Women*, DVD; *presentations:* People of the Smokies: Gone But Not Forgotten; Medicine Women of the Smokies and others.

Every effort has been made to provide an accurate portrayal of facts and individuals who made the Smoky Mountains their homes during the late 1800s-early 1900s and those who played a role in helping create Great Smoky Mountains National Park. Anyone who has new information should contact the publisher to add to the historical record and cultural heritage of this region and these people as portrayed here.

Smoky Mountain Publishers, POB 684, Alcoa, TN 37701

DEDICATION

This book is dedicated to all those who lived in the Smoky Mountains and gave up their homes, land and way of life so Great Smoky Mountains National Park could be formed and made available to all to visit and enjoy. Telling their stories is a way in which to honor who they were and to consider the effect they had on their families, neighbors and communities.

CONTENTS

ACKNOWLEDGMENTS

Thanks to all who shared stories about themselves and their ancestors, especially those who belong to groups dedicated to the preservation of the cultural heritage of the people of the Smoky Mountains. Members of Cades Cove Preservation Association have especially been helpful and generous and include Ruth Davis and her mother, Lois Shuler Caughron; the late Dave Post; Larry Sparks; Inez and Earl Adams. Others include Park Librarian Annette Hardigan; Anne Bridges & Ken Wise, University of Tennessee; Betty Boone Best, Blount County Genealogical Society; Cherl Henderson, East Tennessee Historical Society; authors Margaret & J. C. McCaulley and Lendell Abbott of Maryville. In addition, the work of Linda Weaver as designer proved invaluable, as always. Most of all, I owe thanks to Kathleen Puckett for her support and encouragement in helping bring this and so many other endeavors into reality.

1 IN THE BEGINNING:
FACT, LEGEND & EMINENT DOMAIN

Great Smoky Mountains National Park straddles the ridges of the Smoky Mountains between East Tennessee and Western North Carolina. GSMNP is the most visited of all U. S. national parks, drawing about nine million visitors each year. Its history is that of a coveted land, eventually bought by the two states from individuals and lumber companies with the help of school children and millionaires. The U. S. National Park Service fashioned the land into a Park based on the pioneer era of the people of the Smokies and on the parks of the western U. S. This is the story of how it began, a story of vision, daring and heartbreak.

Establishment of Great Smoky Mountains National Park in the mountains of East Tennessee and Western North Carolina in the 1930s created much conflict among many of the individuals personally involved, especially those whose land was needed to help form the Park. For generations, they or their ancestors settled the land, built cabins and barns, grown crops and raised children. Giving up their land was a hard and bitter pill for some to swallow, especially for something called a "national park."

Most people knew little at that time about the idea of national parks or of conservation of land. National parks only existed in the west, carved out of land already owned by the federal government. The land in the east had to be taken through offers of payment based on an appraisal, or, failing that, through the process of eminent domain; in other words, condemning the land, then taking it. The state still had to pay for land it condemned whether or not the individual agreed. For people living in the Smoky Mountains, the idea of the government taking their land in order to "give it back" to the wilderness was difficult to understand after all the hard work, blood, sweat and tears they and their ancestors had poured into creating homes and communities there.

The two states each appointed a Park commission or committee and gave them authority to condemn the land they wanted to acquire for the Park if the owners weren't willing to sell. One of the questions that arose in the court case brought by land-owner John W. Oliver of Cades Cove, Tenn., who didn't want to sell his land to the states was whether or not one government body (the state) had the right to condemn property they planned to turn over to another government body. Such a question was asked in the case filed in Blount County, Tenn., by John W. Oliver regarding the Tennessee Park Commission's ability to take more than 300 acres of land he owned in Cades Cove and then turn it over to the Federal Government to be included in the planned National Park.

John W. Oliver teaches school in Cades Cove, Tenn., in 1901.
(Courtesy, National Park Service)

Finally, the Tennessee State Supreme Court affirmed that, yes, the state did have such a right. When Oliver eventually tried to appeal that decision, the Supreme Court stated that the basic constitutional question about the state's right to use eminent domain to acquire property in Cades Cove for the Park was deemed settled and could not be appealed (Dunn, p.250, 1988.) Oliver is said to have realized he was fighting a losing battle but kept going for more than six years in the courts including three appeals to the Tennessee State Supreme Court.

After the constitutional issue was settled, he pursued the question of the value given his property. In August of 1931 a jury of view placed a value of $10,090 on Oliver's property, less than its true worth. In June of 1934, a jury of 12 agreed and assessed the value of Oliver's property at $17,000. Another year later on May 9, the Tennessee Court of Appeals in Knoxville affirmed that value and added interest of $807.51.

Once this question was settled, there were no further barriers to the Park Commission's acquiring property for the Park. They moved quickly and began forcing the sale of homes and farms throughout the Cove.

By the end of 1929, the Park Commission had bought half the farms in the Cove, about 52. Other areas of the Smokies within the planned Park boundaries met the same fate.

If Oliver had won his case on the constitutional issue of a state's right to act on behalf of the federal government, many other Covites would have most likely quickly followed his example and filed suit against the Commission in their own behalf. Probably, that would have signaled the end of the national park movement in the Smoky Mountains. As it was, the Park Commission was able to move quickly without fear of any legal restrictions. Ironically, had this land not been folded into the Park area, both Cades Cove, Tenn., and Cataloochee, N.C. as well as other areas of the Smokies, would now most likely resemble the heavily trafficked, crowded commercial areas of Pigeon Forge and Gatlinburg in Tennessee. Rows of condos or cabins would dot the hillsides, water Parks and t-shirt shops would beckon from the roadsides. Even though these facilities bring many visitors and increase the financial benefit to people living in the area surrounding the Park, many people now see the use of eminent domain in acquiring land to add to the Park as eventually having a good result.

Purchase of the land was done in the midst of the Great Depression of the 1920s and 30s when bank failures were at an all-time high. At least some of the individuals who sold their land in the Smokies lost the money they were paid when they put it into a bank (First National Bank of Maryville in 1933, for example) and lost their money or the land they'd bought since leaving their mountain homes.

Even more tragic when families moved out of the mountains, perhaps, was the loss of their community support systems. It seemed especially difficult for women. They had grown to depend on one another in their communities for help from their family and neighbors to join them in chore sharing activities like quilting parties and corn shuckings, as well as with childbirth, illnesses and death. Whole communities came together for barn raisings and to share in the labor of harvesting crops. When individual families moved into areas outside the Park, often they were far from any of the family and neighbors of the coves and hollows of the hills. They had to find strangers to perform services for them (and pay for their services) that they and their neighbors had formerly done for each other or together.

Tenant farmers were another group that removal from the Park hit especially hard, people who didn't own the land, but who worked the land for a share of the crops. In mountain communities such as Cades Cove, these individuals were typically related to the property owners and received care and concern of others nearby who were family members. Once they left the Cove, often with many children, they were thrown into a miserable existence with no resources and little chance of acquiring them during the worst economic downturn in the history of the country. Parents could no longer provide for their children in their own home. Some sent their younger children to live with other family members, mostly older

5

children who'd married and formed their own families. Many such families were never reunited in one place and never recovered economically.

Thus, on a personal, individual level it was a tragic loss for many people. Some say a few of the older folks who left their mountain homes grieved themselves to death over their loss. Some of the younger folks were said to have left gladly, happy to seek new opportunities elsewhere. Some of those left Tennessee and North Carolina and headed for places like Detroit to seek jobs. However, even when they found jobs, many of these people soon traveled back to their homeland in the south. The weather was too cold and the people too different. The love of home place said to be characteristic of people of Appalachia played a role, too, in drawing them "back home."

Author Wilma Dykeman put it this way:

> Tennesseans...have tended to bear a strong allegiance to their places. Perhaps this sense was embedded early and firmly by the fact that, for long generations Tennesseans were an outdoor people. True not only for hunters, trappers, surveyors, farmers, lumbermen, but for most of the professionals.... Preachers "pastured" several churches, or followed arduous circuits in their struggle to tame the unfettered spirits of a civilization in the shaping. Merchants – long trips by horseback, then by wagon... Doctors threw their saddlebags across a sturdy horse...rode in sleet or sun to tend the sick and afflicted, while lawyers traveled to many parts of the state in their bouts to heal society's ills and individuals conflicts (Dykeman, 1975).

These "outdoor" people didn't seem to fare too well in the confines of an industrial mold. So, it's not surprising that many headed back to the southern mountains they considered home.

U.S. Senator Lawrence D. Tyson (D-Tennessee)
(Courtesy, www.wikipedia.org.org)

What seemed like betrayal by public officials was another burden the mountain people carried with them as they left their homes.

U.S. Senator Lawrence D. Tyson (D-Tennessee) issued a statement in 1926 in which he said no person would be "compelled to move or in any way to be disturbed –Congress can pass no bill whatever that can in any way take away the land of any citizen." With this statement, Tyson assured those who lived in the mountains they wouldn't be forced to move and sponsored legislation authorizing formation of Great Smoky Mountains National Park. Likewise, Tennessee Governor Austin Peay told those who lived within the boundaries set for the park they wouldn't be forced to leave and that they "need have no alarm. Such evictions would be a blot upon the state that the barbarism of the Huns could not match."

Peay very much favored formation of GSMNP as well as a game preserve at Reelfoot Lake in west Tennessee. In spite of such statements, these communities were considered by some to have been included as part of the Park all along. Even so, official statements to the contrary lulled home owners in these areas into believing they had nothing to worry about and in turn, nothing to fight about, according to historian Margaret Lynn Brown (Brown, 2000). When they realized their lands were in jeopardy, many wrote pleading letters to anyone they thought could make a difference. Sadly, for them, it was too late. The dye had been cast.

An Elkmont cabin, used as a stable by Alice Margaret Morier, third wife of Col. W. B. Townsend, Little River Lumber Company. *(Courtesy, National Park Service)*

The smaller tracts such as the 1,200 farms and more than 5,000 lots and summer homes continued to be more troublesome and challenging as far as purchase of the land for the Park was concerned. Many of these were smaller lots won in a promotion. Many individuals hadn't paid taxes on these lots and were difficult to find. Yet, the state had to locate the owners, then survey, appraise and buy the lots, a process that took more than 10 years to finish. Eventually, all landowners had to settle for a negotiated amount. Some agreed to take less money if they could remain on the land with a lease. Folks in the Elkmont area were among those who accepted leases on the land they owned and were able to extend their leases until 1992, with two not expiring until 2001.

Their ability to acquire extensions on these properties created some conflict with people whose leases weren't extended on their properties. Later, the Park Service decided to end Elkmont leases and to allow the Elkmont cabins and the Wonderland Hotel to fall into disrepair. The decay of these structures created an outcry among those who felt this was a blatant disregard for preservation of a fondly remembered historical period in the Smokies. The area had begun as a "Gentlemen's Hunting Club" where judges, doctors, lawyers and other well-to-do men came to hunt and fish on weekends. Soon their families began to join them, staying during the weeks to escape the heat of the cities. It became a place for affluent Knoxville families and famous people, such as Charles Darwin and William Faulkner, to come to enjoy nature and to escape oppressive urban summers. The present day campground exists where the original town of Elkmont was located and was at one time the largest town in Sevier County.

However, the hotel and several cabins were placed on the National Historic Register, giving them a special status. Eventually, after the Wonderland fell in 1993 and many of the cabins were beyond repair, a decision was made to restore 18 of the remaining cabins and the Appalachian Club building with all others to be torn down.

In addition to individual land owners, some 18 lumber and pulpwood companies owned about 85 percent of the larger tracts of land set to be bought for the Park in the Smokies (Campbell, 1969). Lumbermen were among those who didn't have a positive view of the formation of a National Park in the Smokies, at least not for their industry. In general, they were in favor of the area being a national forest so they could continue to harvest lumber, which they could not do if it were a national park. Still, they understood it would be only a matter of time even without formation of a national park before they would have to leave the southern woodlands. For one thing, most of the prime areas of timber had already been cut and were in reforestation. Even so, about one-third of the area was still primeval forest and would have provided several more years of clear-cutting. Lumbermen must have felt they could buy time to cut more of the forest still left by resisting the government, at least long enough to allow them to cut and haul away more board feet of timber.

Col. W. B. Townsend of Little River Company in Townsend, Tenn., headed one of those lumber companies. Even while the location of the next national park was being decided, Austin Peay (Democrat) ran for governor of Tennessee and was for the idea of the Smokies becoming a national park. In fact, he said he'd make it a state park, if it didn't become a national one (Campbell, 1969).

To show he was serious, he placed an option to buy the first large tract of land (more than 76,000 acres) from Col. Townsend for $273,557. Townsend had already cut timber from most of it, but his company was still cutting. The later version of the purchase allowed this company to continue cutting another 15 years.

Tennessee Gov. Austin Peay. Democrat, held office 1923-1927. (Courtesy, National Park Service)

For many, establishment of the Park was a sad ending to years of living and working in the "blue smoke" mountains. An examination of the history of the Smokies shows this wasn't the only time one group of individuals was forced to leave the area by another group of individuals. Such "settlings and forced un-settlings" have happened from the very beginning of human occupation of the land.

However, over time, many Smokies residents who'd opposed the coming of the Park, admitted it had probably been a good thing and saved the very land they loved as they knew it when they lived there. Even though homes and other buildings are gone, they can still find their way around the old homesteads, visit churches and cemeteries and "soak in the mountains."

2 The Early Western Frontier

The first European traders and settlers knew the states of Kentucky, Tennessee and Western North Carolina as the Western Frontier. These lands were considered a true wilderness then, wild and untamed, full of deer, bear, wolves, otters, panthers and even bison. Masses of truly old growth forest towered over rushing rivers and tumbling waterfalls that crashed to the rocks below.

In spite of all that, this "Western Frontier" was far from being a true untamed wilderness and hasn't been since humans came into its forests and crossed its streams and rivers. As historian Margaret Lynn Brown points out in *Wild, Wild East*, natives changed the environment to suit themselves, planting and cultivating crops, cutting timber to build their homes, diverting water in order to catch fish, hunting some animals and taming or domesticating others. Admittedly, such environmental changes were done on a much smaller scale than occurred later as more immigrants and lumber companies poured into the region, changing and fashioning the land to their own needs.

Brown contends the Smoky Mountains were "less a wilderness than a pastoral landscape," a created wilderness if you will, created by Native Americans as well as later by European arrivals. Brown's characterization of the Smokies as a created wilderness runs afoul of the image most Americans had (and many still have) of this region as a "pristine wilderness." But, though the Smokies seem like a true wilderness even today, with its many wild animals and few humans inhabiting forbidding terrain of craggy, steep mountains and deep hollows, it was shaped by humans long before it became part of the United States.

But this image of a wild, untamed wilderness surrounded by wonderfully scenic and majestic mountains as well as the fear all this was being destroyed by logging drew attention to the region and eventually caused it to become a National Park. The early 1900s became a time of the unsettling of this region, already with a long history of settlement by many groups at various times, each of which were eventually replaced by another group who wanted the same lands.

Ironically, those living in the region during the late 1800s were among those who first saw the mountains as worthy of being set aside as public lands. And others living there were among the last to let go of their own piece of these lands.

Some of these settlers left willingly. Some expressed their opinion about the taking of their land for a park on signs posted where land agents assigned to buy their land would pass by and see them. One sign addressed Colonel David Chapman, one of the leaders of the Park movement.

Handmade and unpainted, the three-foot sign was posted at the point where Rich Mountain Road joins the Loop Road in Cades Cove: "Colonel Chapman. You and hoast are notfy, let the Cove people alone. Get out. Get gone. 40 M. limit" (Campbell, 1969). The word "hoast" on the sign is thought to refer to the men who came into the Smokies to buy land from area residents for use as a park. The "40 M. limit" mentioned on the sign is said to be a way of telling Chapman to "come no closer than 40 miles to Cades Cove—the distance between Knoxville and the Cove by the old route." Chapman reported, too, that he had received phone calls telling him he would "spend the next night in hell" if he came into the Cove again. All of which shows how much antagonism there was among some people about the takeover of Cove land for use as part of the planned park.

One of the things that aggravated this feeling, especially among individuals living in Cades Cove, was their perception of a promise made by many officials not to include the settled land of Cades Cove as part of the Park.

As Brown pointed out, "Colonel Chapman repeatedly said to the media that people would not be forced out of their homes." It was reported in the *Knoxville Free Press* that they (park promoters) wanted a park, but wouldn't "be a party to visiting upon the people of the park area such a cold-blooded fate as that planned to deprive them of the only home they know" (Brown, Margaret L., 2000).

Because of statements such as these, residents of Cades Cove in Tennessee and Cataloochee in North Carolina were caught off guard, soothed into feeling as though they were safe from seizure of their lands by the state for a national park. The people of Cataloochee didn't believe it when the announcement was made at church one Sunday. People of the area didn't understand what a national park was. After all, they had worked hard to tame the land, to cultivate it, build homes on it and raise their families there. Surely, all their efforts wouldn't be allowed to disappear back into the very wilderness they had fought back through hard work and determination.

And, yet, that was the vision of some of those favoring a park. Some wanted it once again to be a land with no sign of human habitation, only wild animals to witness hikers and campers. The push-and-pull between these two groups about whether GSMNP was to be a wilderness or a place created for the enjoyment of people has continued to the present day. Both actually are the directives toward national parks as set out by Congressional legislation.

Anne M. & Willis P. Davis
(Courtesy, National Park Service)

The Great Smoky Mountains National Park was thus a long time coming and took many people to push it through. It was an idea suggested by Anne M. Davis, wife of Willis P. Davis, president of Knoxville Iron Company, after she and her husband visited national parks out west. Both worked tirelessly to bring this vision into reality along with Col. David C. Chapman, whose family ran a Knoxville wholesale drug company, and Ben Morton, mayor of Knoxville. Chapman and the Davises had a summer place in Elkmont. Each proved to be a special champion for the park movement. Morton, son of the late Dr. B. A. Morton, a well-loved doctor in Maryville (Campbell, 1960), helped persuade some Cades Cove people to sell their land, or accept a lease so they could remain on their land.

However, others had the idea of the Smokies as a national park as early as the late 1800s. On Oct. 29, 1885, Dr. Henry O. Marcy, a Boston physician, addressed the American Academy of Medicine in New York City and suggested the higher ranges of the Smokies should be secured for use as a national park. Four years later, Dr. Chas P. Ambler of North Carolina pushed for a national park in the region. In Feb. 9, 1893, the North Carolina legislature passed a resolution in favor of a park. A year later, John Henderson of North Carolina presented a petition for a park to the U.S. House of Representatives. However, the measure died in committee (Givens, 1978).

Anne M. Davis was serving as a representative in the Tennessee Legislature in 1925, one of the first women elected to the Legislature. Governor Peay gave her the honor of presenting a bill supporting the purchase of land for preservation. The first bill supporting a Smokies national park in Tennessee was defeated because of lobbyists representing the timber industry (Brown, Fred. KNS, Jan. 25, 2009). However, Davis worked with Morton and Chapman to develop a plan to make the purchase using Knoxville taxpayer money rather than State taxpayer money. Members of Knoxville's City Council agreed to pay one-third of the cost of land available from Little River Lumber Company in Townsend. Governor Peay supported the idea and eventually, Col. W. B. Townsend sold his holdings in the Smoky Mountains for $3.57 an acre or a total of

$273, 557. Townsend's agreement to sell allowed him to cut timber for an additional 15 years.

It was not until 1926 that President Calvin Coolidge signed the bill that approved creation of a national park in the region. That bill required 150,000 acres of land be accumulated for park designation. In this case, the land had to be bought from individuals and logging companies by the states, and then turned over to the National Park Service. The states couldn't use taxpayer money to buy the land. Donations came in the form of pennies from schoolchildren and millions from others, such as John D. Rockefeller.

Home of the Walker Sisters, Little Greenbrier. (Courtesy, wikipedia.org)

In July of 1930, the Federal government accepted title to 158,816 acres in the proposed area for the Park. In October of 1935, the Federal government accepted title to additional land in the region, increasing the total to more than 400,000 acres, or the minimum set by Congress.

Logging on the Tennessee side of the Smokies ended. At that time, too, the area was given full national park status. The Park Service did allow residents of the Park in those areas not scheduled for immediate development to sell their land to the government, and lease it back. The Walker sisters in Little Greenbrier in East Tennessee were among those who were able to do this and lived in their cabin until the 1960s, when the last living sister, Louisa (pronounced Loo-i-sa), died. All of the sisters, including Caroline and her husband Jim Shelton, are buried in Mattox Cemetery in Wears Valley. However, many other families weren't happy with the lease agreements because of restrictions placed on them.

"They tell me I can't break a twig, nor pull a flower, after there's a Park. Nor can I fish with bait, nor kill a boomer [squirrel], nor bear on land owned by my pap, and gandpapa and his pap before him" (Brown, Margaret L., 2000). On the other hand, during those early days, Park Service personnel themselves were bent on killing snakes wherever they found them.

Many of the former residents continued to go into Park lands to hunt and fish (both illegal) and to visit and care for the cemeteries. Even a few who weren't former residents decided to take advantage of the empty buildings and moved in. The Park Service took steps to keep former residents and 'undesirables" such as moon-shiners and prostitutes from moving into these homes by removing stoves and tearing down chimneys as well as tearing down or burning many of the buildings.

In the end, Cades Cove was the only major settled area in East Tennessee to become part of the new National Park. An initial proposal for the boundaries of the National Park in East Tennessee had included the communities of Wear's Cove, Walden's Creek and Tuckaleechee Cove, or

Townsend. However, enough people who lived in these regions were able to make themselves heard loudly enough that these areas were deleted from the final Park plan.

Other settled areas that eventually became part of the Park included every other part of the Smokies except for the high mountain peaks. Cades Cove, Elkmont, Greenbrier, Sugarlands, Big Creek, Cataloochee, Deep Creek, Forney Creek, Hazel Creek, Proctor, Eagle Creek—all areas where people had lived, worked and raised their families, built homes and churches and established cemeteries.

Some public services kept going even after the Park was established. In December of 1935, some 21 families still in Cades Cove received notice to vacate by Jan. 1, 1936. Mail delivery in the Cove stopped in 1940, but the Post Office stayed open until Oct. 31, 1947. Most people left by 1934, but elections for local officials continued through 1936. Cable School in Cades Cove continued until 1943-44 (Dunn, 1988).

In North Carolina, 200 families were still living in the Park in 1940. However, that was not to last. When the U.S. entered World War II, all Federal government efforts, even creating a national park, seemed to become part of the war effort (Brown, Margaret L. 2000). To that end, the Tennessee Valley Authority began building Fontana Dam to produce hydroelectric power, especially for use by Alcoa Aluminum Company in Maryville, Tenn. TVA bought another 55,000 acres, almost 12,000 of which were flooded to create Fontana Lake. More than 1,300 families were relocated. The Aluminum Company of America had already bought 15,000 acres in the mountains with an eye toward building a dam on the Little Tennessee River in North Carolina.

Part of the mandate to TVA by the U.S. Congress was to improve flood control and economic conditions in the region. Not much mention was made of the fact that at least some of the flooding experienced in Western North Carolina resulted from the intensive logging that had stripped the slopes of the mountains (Brown, Margaret L., 2000).

At any rate, the war pushed everyone to come together and in August of 1941, TVA and ALCOA signed an agreement under which ALCOA agreed to give TVA the 15,000 acres it bought in the region in exchange for receiving whatever electric power it needed. TVA agreed to buy the rest of the more than 53,000 acres needed for the project and, possibly most importantly, to foot the $70 million it was going to cost to build the dam. Work on the dam began Jan. 8, 1942, and ended Feb. 16, 1945. About 7,276 acres were cleared. Total cost for the project came to $912,000. Man hours worked came to more than 1.5 million, with people working six-day/48-hour weeks.

The war ended before the dam and Fontana Lake were actually completed. During the building of the dam, TVA was given a duty to help lesson the hardships brought to the 216 families residing in the area at the time. The flooding needed to form Fontana Lake cut off the only public road or means of access to these families. The only way to travel to the north shore area was by boat, by horseback or on foot. It was as though the region was changed back to pioneer days.

In July of 1943, the State of North Carolina paid $100,000 to TVA to help acquire the land needed for the dam and reservoir. Swain County was to be paid $400,000 to retire the bonds used to build NC State Road 288 which served the area to the north of Little Tennessee River. TVA transferred the property they acquired to the National Park Service on

March 31, 1948. A road to replace NC No. 288 was begun from Bryson City along the North Shore of Fontana Lake, but never finished and acquired the nickname, "The Road to Nowhere." The issue of whether to complete the road or not was settled in 2010 when the U. S. Senator from North Carolina, Heath Shuler, put his support behind not finishing the road but paying the money owed to the State of North Carolina. Former Smoky Mountain residents had fought for building of the road for nearly 50 years.

Most were concerned their ability to visit cemeteries on the North Shore of Fontana Lake wouldn't continue if a road weren't built to replace the one they'd lost to the lake. Since that time, an agreement between TVA and the Park Service allows people to visit the cemeteries by providing boats to ferry visitors across the lake from April through October each Sunday. A schedule of visits is available on the web site of North Shore Cemetery Association (http://northshorecemeteries.com/).

TVA records show the reservoir of Fontana covered more than 10,000 acres, destroyed at least six established towns, and forced the relocation of 11 cemeteries with more than 1,000 graves. Individuals from four cemeteries (Judson, Montheith, Hyde and Delozier) were moved to Lauada, a cemetery created by TVA located on US 19 south of Bryson City, N.C. In 1945 when TVA built Fontana Dam, 13 churches were lost from the rolls of the Tennessee Baptist Association: Bone Valley, Cable Branch, Bushnell, Chambers Creek, Fontana, Epps Springs, Forney's Creek, Fontana Mines, Judson, Powells Branch, Rhymers, Tennessee River and Almond (later rebuilt). Most of these were on the north shore of Little Tennessee and Tuckasegee Rivers.

Cades Cove Missionary Baptist
Church *(Courtesy, Gail Palmer)*

In Tennessee, the effects of the newly formed Park also were felt. The
Cades Cove Primitive Baptist Church maintained its membership into the
1960s. Church members had secured the right in 1940 to a yearly lease.
The other Cove churches disbanded as their members left.

Daniel Lawson, who deeded the land for the Hopewell Methodist
Church, South and Cemetery in Cades Cove to "God Almighty," told those
who negotiated purchase of land in the Park that they should "go negotiate
with God, He owns it" (Burns, 1995). The church, often called the Lawson
Chapel and built by Lawson after his return from the Civil War, is no
longer standing. Some people say he didn't serve in either army during the
Civil War, but stayed in the Cove and tended a field far up a hollow near
his home that was far enough away that few soldiers would venture up the
mountain to search for him (Adams, interview, 2011). The cemetery has
26 graves and is east of the Lawson cabin and barn on the back side of the
loop road in Cades Cove.

The people all eventually left their mountain homes, even though some
of them settled close by. Some buildings including cantilevered barns were

22

left in Cades Cove and Cataloochee and a few other areas of the Park, especially buildings representative of the pioneer era. In other areas the buildings were sold for scrap or burned (Van West, 1998).

Between 1931 and 1940 Federal and State agencies built amenities for tourists, as many as 800 miles of trails and four major road systems within Park boundaries (Brown, Magaret L. 2000).

The state and federal governments together created something new on the ancient mountains, a scene, a rustic image or a vision of what America should be—"they revised and adulterated history in a way that suited their own interests and tourists' aesthetics" (Brown, Margaret L. 2000). The Park became a modern playground for hikers, campers, horseback riders and fishermen, managed by the government.

The people responded. They began coming to "their" Park as quickly as it was built. In the Depression in June of 1934, more than 40,000 people came from 40 states and one foreign country. Six years later, again in June, more than 128,000 people came to the Smokies. Almost half of them came from outside Tennessee and North Carolina. Traffic became a concern and the word "bottleneck" began to be used to describe summer traffic between Pigeon Forge and Gatlinburg.

The Great Smoky Mountains National Park was a success, at least in terms of popularity with the public. People were hungry for a chance to be in a natural, wilderness setting, even though for many it was only a drive-through experience. The lumber companies were long gone along with the residents. The sound of the steam-whistle of Shay engines moving up and down the sides of the mountains, the wheels of rail cars straining and moaning under their loads along with the peal of church bells sounding across the valleys had been replaced by the sound of automobile engines gearing up as cars wound slowly around the 11-miles of paved road surrounding the valley of Cades Cove, along Newfound Gap Road and Roaring Fork Trail, any paved road to be found within Great Smoky Mountains National Park, and a few unpaved roads. Nearly nine million visitors come to this Park each year, some only to drive through, others to hike many of the nearly 900 trails within Great Smoky Mountains National Park. Some people come back year after year. Others are inspired to move to one of the communities around the Park so they can visit more areas of the Park more often.

Cades Cove, Cataloochee, Elkmont and other places in the Smokies are populated once again with deer, coyote and black bear.

Smoky Mountains black bear.
(Courtesy, National Park Service)

3 <u>Thar's Gold in Them Hills</u>

Europeans were drawn to these mountains years before the first permanent white settlers came. In 1540, Spanish explorer Hernando De Soto came through the Smoky Mountains. Then governor of Cuba, De Soto landed seven ships with 600 men near Tampa, Fla. (Blackmun, 1977). He is thought to have headed the first European expedition to explore what is now the southeastern U.S. One theory says De Soto traveled from Florida's west coast, north into Georgia, and then across the southern tip of the Smokies into the Carolinas. Some historians think he may have gone north into the Carolinas, crossed back into Tennessee, and then down through the Tennessee Valley.

Long before any European settlers set foot on the American continent, several native tribes claimed the valleys to the east and west of the mountain ranges in Tennessee and Western North Carolina as their hunting grounds. Most of the year, they lived in villages in the valleys on either side of the southern Appalachians, and sent hunting parties into and across the mountains. They walked the steep, winding trails and hunted the abundant game living in the deep, virgin forests.

During De Soto's journey, he and his men came in contact with American Indians living in the area at that time. The name Cherokee first appeared in the writings of De Soto's historian. In an effort to duplicate what he thought he'd heard, the historian wrote their tribal name as "chalaque." After another 100 years passed, the French wrote the name as "Cheraqui." Finally, the English spelled it "Cherokee" and this version stuck (Blackmun, 1977).

The Cherokee, though, called themselves Yun'wiya or Ani Yun'wiya, "principle people." They are thought to have once been part of the Delaware Indians and the Iroquois, a tribe located in the north.

Huts built by Cherokee existed on the valley floor of Cades Cove when the first European settlers came there. Descendents say one such hut was behind the Dan Lawson barn on the backside of the loop road. Evidence of their settlements have been discovered along the banks of Little River running through Townsend, Tenn., and other areas of the land around the edges of the Smokies, such as Cataloochee. The settlements revealed by archeological digs in Townsend were studied and photographed, then with the blessing of members of the Cherokee tribe, were covered with concrete as part of U. S. Highway 321. A state highway sign marks the area and gives more information about the discovery.

The search for gold was one of the driving forces behind De Soto's visit to the area. Although he found no gold on this trip, some 27 years later, another Spaniard, Juan Pardo, did find gold—and silver—somewhere in the region visited by De Soto (Blackmun, 1977). For more than 125 years after that, small groups of Spaniards came into the area east and west of the Blue Ridge Mountains to mine for gold and silver.

Later, Dr. Calvin Post of Cades Cove searched for gold, too. He is said to have found copper in North Carolina but no gold, even though he called an area in Cades Cove that he worked "El Dorado."

In 1629, almost 90 years after De Soto came through the region, English King Charles I gave the lands of the entire Cherokee nation to his friend Attorney General Sir Robert Heath (Blackmun, 1977). Heath was supposed to send settlers to this new colony of Carolina (a Latinized form of the name, Charles). After 20 years, the grant was voided. Three years after that, Charles II gave the Heath grant to eight of his lords, known as proprietors. Some settlements were established in Carolina, mostly on the coast around Charlestown.

During the early 1700s, trappers and traders crept into the Western Frontier from the Carolinas and surrounding areas, even though American Indians still claimed the land. Some white traders settled in American Indian villages, some took Indian wives. The Indians and traders first followed animal trails into the area, then wagons followed them. Eventually, trails became roads, then turnpikes.

Before the late 1700s, both mountains and Indians effectively blocked the way into the Smokies to the colonists of the Carolinas, Maryland and Virginia. However, many European settlers were anxious to go into the alluring, empty lands to the west.

4 <u>They Came, They Stayed</u>

Traders, hunters and trappers who came into the region in the early periods weren't interested in owning land. However, a different breed of pioneers came into and across the mountains from 1759 to 1771, so much so that the population of North Carolina doubled with the thousands of immigrants who came from Germany, Switzerland, Ireland, France, Scotland and England or from Maryland, Pennsylvania, Virginia or the coasts of the Carolinas.

The first white settlers didn't appear west of the Blue Ridge Mountains until after the Revolutionary War which ended in 1783 (Morley, 1913). Many were soldiers who were given land grants in payment for their services during the war. Some of the settlers came into the area during the War, liked what they saw, and came back after the war. Many settlers originally came from England or were of English descent, but large numbers of Scotch-Irish came from Virginia. Cherokee County, now the westernmost county in North Carolina, was actually one of the last areas of that state to be settled by whites. Most of the Europeans settled in the valleys rather than the hills or mountains. The northern area of Western

North Carolina, on the other hand, later lured people from the coast to visit the cooler mountains during the summers to escape the hot, humid lowlands.

From time to time, as newcomers pushed into the area, a number of treaties or agreements were made between the English (and later, Americans) and the Indians. Some worked and were honored, at least for a time. Mostly, though, treaties were made and then broken by both parties. As the years passed, Indians gave up more and more of their land. Indians and the settlers fought back and forth with first one, then the other on the attack. Eventually, armed troops went through Cherokee towns, destroying them as they went.

The war between the English and the Cherokee ended November 19, 1761, and the Cherokee never fully recovered. Out of an estimated 64 Cherokee towns, about 20 remained, Almost all crops were destroyed on the brink of winter. Many Cherokee starved that year. Still, some were willing to learn the white man's ways, possibly as a form of what they thought would be self-preservation. Many bought farms, went to the white man's schools and were converted in the white man's churches, i.e. became as much like the whites as they could. Some Cherokee practices were even woven into their church cultures.

Whites continued to push into the region, building forts and clearing land. In 1785, White's Fort was built in Knoxville in East Tennessee. About the same time, Samuel Wear built a fort at the mouth of Walden's Creek in Pigeon Forge (Trout, 1984).

The Smokies offered these newcomers a vision of land where they could settle, where they could raise a family and make a living, even though many of those drawn to settle in the central Appalachians were unskilled or semiskilled workers. Some of those who came to the colonies from England, Ireland, Scotland, Germany and other countries found some conditions along the coastal areas or in the Piedmont not to their liking, especially the heavy taxes Virginia levied to support the Episcopal Church. Many found the strict formality and lack of emotionalism of the Episcopal service not very appealing (Cressman, 1994). Some of these people had come into the New World as indentured servants or were children kidnapped from England. Whatever their reasons, they fled into the mountains where there were no taxes and few churches, especially state-supported ones.

Later, churches became a vital part of some communities and were primarily Baptist. Preachers of this religion came from the congregation, called by God to preach. There were few other requirements for men to become Baptist ministers in the mountain churches. Methodists came next and served many communities by offering the services of circuit riding preachers, men who rode the mountains with a Bible in one hand and a rifle in the other. Presbyterians played a role, too, although later outnumbered by Methodists, and especially by Baptists.

Those who came to the mountains found life a hard and continuous struggle. The National Park Service auto-tour booklet describing the Ephraim Bales home in Roaring Fork in Gatlinburg gives some idea of what life may have been like for some settlers, especially in their first houses.

"Ephraim Bales . . . his wife and their nine children lived crammed into this dogtrot cabin . . . individual privacy was something these people knew little about . . . split log floors were drafty and allowed an occasional snake to slide in . . . small doors conserved heat . . . the only window is the 'granny hole,' which looks out on the family pantry—the corn crib . . . in front of the hearth is the 'tater' hole . . . it was a simple matter to lift a puncheon (floor board), withdraw some potatoes and toss them into the ashes to bake . . . .Life for the Bales family was as sparse and hard as the ground around them" (GSMNPS auto-tour booklet).

Ephraim Bales cabin, Roaring Fork, Gatlinburg.
(Courtesy wikipedia.org.org)

The Bales family is thought to have lived in Roaring Fork 1865-1925, but their lives probably mirrored in many ways the lives of those who came to the region earlier. On the plus side, many of those who survived such a harsh life became sturdy, self-reliant, independent individuals. It's thought that the perception of themselves as self-reliant helped determine their religious and political views that, in turn, helped shape the destiny of the area for years after.

By 1729 the mountain section of Carolina became part of North Carolina. The area, though, was more influenced by the laws and government of South Carolina (Blackmun, 1977). In 1789, the State of North Carolina offered the territory to the federal government, which accepted the offer and organized the area as the Territory South of the Ohio. In 1794, the Territory of Tennessee was formed and William Blount appointed governor by President George Washington. In 1795, the Territory of Tennessee became the State of Tennessee. It was the first new state to be admitted to the new union from the western lands given to the federal government by North Carolina. John Sevier was the first elected governor.

John Sevier, Revolutionary War hero, first governor of Tennessee. *(Courtesy, www.wikipedia.org)*.

In order to keep what they considered to be their land, though, the state's citizens had to fight the Cherokee, as well as the weather and the nature of the land itself. Travel was possible only by foot or by horseback on steep and muddy trails and in some areas remained so for many years. For example, one November day in 1800, Methodist Bishop Francis Asbury tried to travel by horse-drawn carriage from Tennessee to Asheville, N.C. The road was so rough and steep that his horse reeled and fell, landing upside down. Horse and carriage were wedged against a tree (Blackmun, 1977). Bishop Asbury had no choice but to leave his horse and carriage and ride another horse the rest of the way.

Bishop Francis Asbury
(Courtesy, wikipedia.org)

The following Sunday, he tried to take a chaise—a smaller, lighter wagon—from north of Asheville to Biltmore, only about five miles. Again the road was so rough he had to swap the chaise for a horse in order to continue his trip. Although the good Bishop had his troubles navigating through the mountains and exclaimed about his difficulties, years later it was suggested that Cataloochee Turnpike in the North Carolina section of the GSMNP be renamed "Asbury Turnpike" because of his many trips back and forth. However, the Park Service decided to retain the historical name of Cataloochee Turnpike (Wilburn, 1943).

5 Apples, Chestnuts, Corn, Grains, Cows, Hogs, Turkeys Market Bound

The mountains gave East Tennessee and Western North Carolina culture many unique characteristics, including some negative ones, such as restricting access to markets. Before the Civil War, though, roads were good enough for East Tennessee to become a source of pork and corn as well as other food commodities for sections of Alabama and Georgia, as well as the plantations of the Carolinas (Groce, 1992). Groce said that Tennessee hogs and corn were inexpensive enough that it was more efficient for people in Alabama, Georgia and Carolina to buy what they needed from Tennessee rather than to produce such commodities themselves. Farmers around Knoxville found it easier and less expensive to feed their grain to hogs, and then drive the hogs into market at Knoxville and other towns. So it was that Knoxville became a trade center to the states of the lower South, the Carolinas and Virginia. About 150-175,000 hogs a year were herded across the mountains into the Carolinas before the Civil War (Groce, 1992). By 1860, Tennessee ranked near the top in production of corn and hogs.

Feeding crops they grew such as grain or corn to animals to maximize their profits wasn't the only way they used such items. Many used corn, grain, apples and peaches to make moonshine, whiskey or brandy. It was a lot easier to carry corn out in a jar, and they made a lot more money than if they'd taken sacks of grain or corn to market. That ended for most Tennessee farmers by 1879, when Federal laws outlawed untaxed liquor and the Tennessee vs. Davis Supreme Court decision gave the feds jurisdiction in prosecuting moon shiners.

This action closed most moonshine making operations in both Tennessee and North Carolina. However, a few refused to stop such a profit-making venture, particularly when they had invested heavily in equipment and crops. Some were killed by competitors or jailed by law officials. Others kept an operation going but most were small and in constant danger of discovery.

Another commodity moved through the mountains "on the hoof," or, in this case, on the wing were turkeys. Herding turkeys through the mountains worked fairly well during the daytime but come dark it was a different story. Turkeys roosted in whatever trees or bushes might be accessible to them. Once settled, they were settled for the night and there was nothing for the herders to do but wait until morning to round up their winged charges. Sometimes herders scattered seed to encourage the turkeys to stay on the trail. Eventually, they made it to market in Knoxville or in Asheville.

Many farmers, some as far away as Knoxville, drove their herds into the mountains up to the balds or mountaintop meadows in the spring. No trees grew here leaving open, grassy fields, perfect for livestock. Men from the mountain communities owned the balds and leased them to the farmers, while other community men served as herders. Gregory Bald and Spence Field are two major balds and were leased by their owners to other farmers. A field above Big Cove in N.C. was owned by the Cherokee and leased to white settlers. Gregory Bald is 3,000 feet above Cades Cove to the southwest (Dunn, 1988). Spence Field is on the state line between Tennessee and North Carolina.

In 1902, farmers grazed cattle on Cherokee land for $10 per year (Brown, Margaret L., 2000). Sometimes, almost 800 cattle grazed their land over the summer. Cataloochee farmers grazed their cattle without a herder, but made the trip once a week to supply the animals with salt left in logs on the ground with holes chopped in them to hold the salt. The animals always came back for the salt, so herders didn't have to look for them. In the fall, herders drove the animals back down the mountains and then to market. Sheep, cows and hogs were generally the animals that were sent to the balds.

Herders such as Tom Sparks stayed in small cabins at Spence Field or Russell Field over the summer. They charged the owners so much per animal. Each owner had his animals marked with ear notches so they could claim them in the fall as they came back down the mountain. Sparks herded cattle for 50 years, usually about 700 cattle, 500 sheep and 50 horses. His was the largest herd. John Gregory herded with Sparks at Spence Field and Russell Place from April 15 to September 15. They charged by the head to take care of the animals: $1 to $1.50 per head for cattle; 0.25 for sheep. Tom Cooper, another herder, had a large barn at Russell Field. Joe Russell is said to have lived and died up there.

Herders sometimes lost animals to predators such as panthers and bears. Wolves left the Eastern Mountains many years before at the first sound of a bloomery forge used in Cades Cove to make iron. One evening, Tom Sparks was on his way up the mountain to Spence Field carrying a sack of salt on his back to put into the salt lick for the animals in his charge. It was dusk as he walked along Anthony Creek Trail

Herder Tom Sparks at Spence Field (*Courtesy, National Park Service*)

He thought he heard someone on the opposite side of the creek and, as was the custom in the mountains, he called out a greeting. No response came, so he kept walking up the trail, heard some one or something coming up the trail behind him. It turned out to the something heavy and it landed on his back. It was a panther. He struggled with the animal and managed to plunge his knife into its left shoulder. The big cat stopped his attack and took off into the darkness. Tom made it to the cabin at Spence Field and tended to his wounds.

Days later, someone told him he'd found a panther not far from Spence Field with a wounded left shoulder and killed it. He thought it might be the same one that had attacked Sparks. Although it's said that was the last panther known to be in the Smokies, a few sightings of panthers have been reported through the years, but none have been substantiated. Some people think if there are any panthers roaming the mountains now, it's animals that have escaped from wildlife preserves or turned loose by their owners when they became unmanageable. Nonetheless, the thought of the eerie sound of the panther's cry is enough to make anyone nervous who has lived in the mountains.

Herders lost animals to the weather, too, if they took their herds to the upper elevations too soon. One year a cold spell caught a herder in North Carolina during a late spring with his sheep and cattle in a blizzard. The sheep survived because it was said they moved around, but the cattle stood their ground and were frozen on the spot. The herders came back later and found the bones of the animals piled together in the valley. The place is known today as Bone Valley.

Nonetheless, the people living in the coves and valleys grew familiar with the sound of bells attached to the animals as they walked to and from the mountaintops. People who lived in the Cove looked forward to the days when the herders walked their animals up the trails to the balds.

Sometimes only the lead animal wore a bell around its neck. Each bell had its own tone and owners recognized the sound their own bell made.

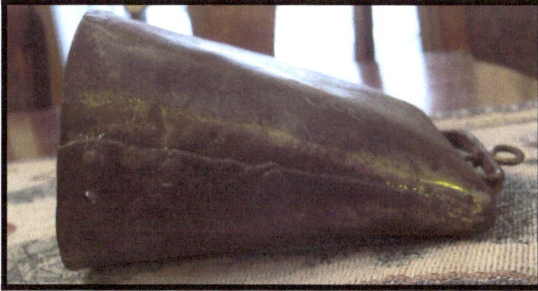

Typical bell used by herders on lead animals. Each bell had a different sound, determined by amount of brass used in them.
(Courtesy, J.C. & Margaret McCaulley, Maryville, Tenn.)

As the sound of the bells echoed across the valley, people knew the livestock were on their way to the top of the mountains to spend the summer, or heading down the mountain in the fall. It was a pleasant and welcome serenade weaving through the trees that signaled the beginning of seasons to the mountain people.

6 <u>Train Whistles Echo & Trees Fall</u>

Still another, more grating sound crashed over the hills and valleys of the Smokies in the late 1800s, the sound of train whistles, axes and saws, metal clanging against metal. These sounds heralded the coming of the lumber industry to the Smokies.

Before the late 1870s, logging was limited to small operations on both sides of the Smoky Mountains, usually a lone sawmill located near waterways so logs could be floated out. With the arrival of men from major lumber companies, men moved the mills to the trees, rather than the trees to the mills (Schmidt and Hooks, 1994).

At that time, tanbark was in great demand for tanning leather. Chestnut, oak and hemlock bark were needed. As a result, the bark was taken and the rest of the tree left where it fell. Bark could be easily packed out on the backs of mules or horses or in wagons. By the 1870s lumber began to be moved by tram, rough platforms mounted on wheels shaped to straddle wooden rails. Men, horses, mules, oxen and gravity helped move trams along the rails to a tannery.

By the 1880s, lumber companies turned their focus toward the South, in particular the Smoky Mountains of East Tennessee and Western North Carolina. They had already cut through the hardwoods around the Great Lakes and began to consider the large, virgin forests of the southern mountains. Several companies and individuals, including Colonel W. B. Townsend, formed the Little River Lumber Company in Townsend, Tennessee, and converged on the southern mountains. Townsend bought thousands of acres on the Tennessee side of the Smokies, while Ritter Lumber Company and Kitchens Lumber Company were but two of those that came into the forests of Western North Carolina.

Served as church, school and movie theatre in logging town of Tremont.
"House of Salvation, Education & Damnation." *(National Park Service)*

During this period, several inventions came along that helped improve the efficiency of the lumber industry and enabled loggers to reach for timber located on the steep, rocky slopes of the Smokies. In 1877, Elmer Shay invented a geared locomotive to use to move logs to the mill. This little engine was ideal for use in the mountains on steep grades and could maneuver heavy loads around sharp curves and over irregular track. The band saw was another important development of the times. The trains brought the timber to the mill and the band saw stood ready to perform high speed cutting of thick logs with very little waste (Schmidt and Hooks, 1994). Another development that helped lead to mass production of timber was the overhead skidder.

A large log being loaded onto a flat car in the Smokies
(*Courtesy, www.wikipedia.org.org*)

This device picked up logs and swung them through the air by cable, loading them onto trains for transport down the mountainsides. It was a quick and efficient method of moving timber down the mountains to the band saw, but it tore up anything on the land in its path on the way down. Mass production techniques of clear cutting led inevitably to mass destruction of the southern forests and created problems with fire caused by sparks landing on brush piles next to the tracks. Inevitably, with nothing left to hold the dirt in place when it rained, floods developed. Rains poured over the barren areas and removed whatever topsoil was left. That meant the soil and what could grow there was changed forever. In parts of NC, smaller trees, such as fire cherry and yellow spruce, grow where Fraser fir and red spruce once stood.

Other changes took place that involved almost every living thing. Schmidt and Hooks point out that it took only about 40 years to clear out the forests in the Little River area of East Tennessee, and, indeed, throughout the southeastern United States. By the 1890s, most of the valuable hardwoods were gone from the lower regions of the mountains (Copeland, 1992). Cherry, ash and walnut were being cut at the higher elevations. Most of the walnut was used to make sewing machine cabinets, something the people of the mountains didn't know existed for home use until much later.

Railroads were built into the mountains to bring lumber out and to take workers in. The workers for the lumber companies were sometimes moved from place-to-place via rail. Their rectangular houses, precursors to the modern day mobile home, could be lifted onto a flatcar and moved to another spot next to the rail line and downloaded to the new location. When timber in that area played out, the boxcars, workers and their families were moved again. Workers paid $3 a month to rent one of these boxcar homes set a few feet from the railroad track.

Many mountain men welcomed these jobs, even though the wages in North Carolina were 12 cents an hour compared to 22 cents per hour earned by men for the same work in the state of Washington. Workers were paid in company script, good only at

the company store. One script, called "dugaloo," was a coin with
the name of the company inscribed on it and a square hole in the
middle. Much of the time, men working for the lumber companies
did, indeed, owe most of what they earned to the company store.

In NC, men could work almost 63 hours each week, compared to
59 or 60 in Washington (Brown, Margaret L., 2000). Should a
worker be injured and unable to work, he and his family were on
their own. Even though a doctor was usually in the lumber camps,
at least on certain days, the workers had to pay for any care they
received.

Logging continued in some parts of the region for many more years. It
wasn't until the area began to be formed into a National Park that logging
stopped. In this way, the formation of the Great Smoky Mountains
National Park kept the mountains from being completely stripped of its
virgin forests, although just barely. The last logs came out of Walker
Valley near Townsend, Tennessee, in 1939. A stand of old growth trees
survived in NC. The lumber company had saved the best for last, a
fortunate decision for proponents of the Park.

Logging in North Carolina ended in the early 1940s when TVA
purchased land to build Fontana Dam. In that state, the Park took some
three-fourths of Swain County's taxable land. Ninety percent of that land
has a slope of 30 degrees or more. When TVA came in and took the land to
build Fontana Dam, they ended a thriving lumber industry and closed
several mines. It had taken W. M. Ritter Company 17 years to cut timber
out of the Hazel Creek tract, which produced 166 million board feet of
lumber. In 1920, the value of the Swain County lumber production was
more than $2 million. TVA shut down two copper mines in the area—one

'n Fontana on Sugar Fork and one at Hazel Creek at Fontana mines. They had produced several million dollars worth of ore.

Fontana Dam, located in Graham County, NC, is 480 feet high and 2,365 feet across the Little Tennessee River. A gravity dam, it is the tallest dam east of the Mississippi and forms Fontana Lake, 29-miles long.
(Courtesy, polarinertia.com/nov03/fontana01.htm)

For people who lived in Western North Carolina, the building of the dams provided jobs, especially after the lumber companies left and the mines closed. Once the dams were completed, though, the jobs ended, the people left.

7 <u>A National Park and How It Grew</u>

The Great Smoky Mountains National Park was thus a long time coming. From the beginning, traveling the road to creation of this Park in the middle of the Eastern part of the country was not a straight-line journey. It was sparked as an idea in the minds of people such as Anne M. Davis and her husband, Willis P., while visiting the National Parks in the West, and traveled through the acquisition battles that created hard feelings between Smoky Mountain land owners and the state and Federal governments, then inevitably moved to the opening of the Park to the public in 1940. It was full of twists and turns and an uncertain outcome. Finally, acceptance came of the Park as a place accessible to everyone,. Reaching this point had taken constant attention and determination by many players for the Park to be established and made available for the use and enjoyment by anyone who could travel to its boundaries. Unlike other national Parks in the U.S., no fees are charged for entry into GSMNP. This was a major feature put into place in the agreement reached between the states and the Federal government as a result of the insistence of land owners in Cades Cove because they wanted assurance they and their descendents could continue to visit their cemeteries whenever they wanted.

In July of 1930, the Federal government accepted title to 158,816 acres in the proposed area for the Park. In October of 1935, title was accepted by the Federal government to additional land in the region, increasing the total to more than 400,000 acres, or the minimum set by Congress. Logging on the Tennessee side of the Smokies ended. At that time, too, the area was given full national Park status.

However, another five years passed before the dedication of the Park by President Franklin D. Roosevelt in 1940. He came to the Smokies and addressed the crowd at Newfound Gap on the state line with one foot in Tennessee and one in North Carolina. The 11 miles of US Hwy 441 from Sugarlands Visitors Center on the outer edge of Gatlinburg to Newfound Gap was lined every thousand feet with members of the Civilian Conservation Corp, or CCC as it was called (Brown, 2000).

President Franklin D. Roosevelt at the 1940 dedication of Great Smoky Mountains National Park. His wife, Eleanor, is fourth from the right. *(Courtesy, National Park Service)*

On the platform with President Roosevelt were Willis P. and Anne M. Davis, who was called Mother of the Park; Cordell Hull, former congressman and U.S. secretary of state; Prentice Cooper, governor of

Tennessee, 1939-1945; and Kenneth McKellar, six-term U.S. senator and promoter of the Tennessee Valley Authority. All of them played important roles in helping establish the Park.

The President's wife, Eleanor, made the trip with him and was at the dedication. On another visit, she spent time at a lodge in Cades Cove, hiking along Forge Creek Road, stopping to take a drink from the clear, cold waters of Forge Creek. The President had planned to join her on that visit, but his Secret Service agents are said to have decided it would be too difficult to move him out of harm's way if anything happened that threatened his safety while he was there. Mrs. Roosevelt made more visits to Cades Cove than any other local and national dignitaries. There is no indication any of the local people connected the idea that the favorable impression on such visitors of the beauty of this area made it almost impossible not to include it inside park boundaries.

Some may see an ironic twist in the fact that many of those whose ancestors came into the region and settled on land first belonging to the American Indians who'd lived and hunted in the area for many years now found themselves evicted from the same lands. However, none of the individuals, neither white settlers nor Cherokee, were recognized at the dedication. Nor were any of them on the platform with President Roosevelt and the other dignitaries (Brown, Margaret L., 2000). It was as though flora and fauna were the only things that had existed in the Smokies.

One family remained in Cades Cove until 1999. Kermit Caughron and his wife, Lois Shuler, stayed in the caretaker's house next to the Lawson cabin on the loop road until Kermit's death at age 87 on Apr. 15, 1999.

Kermit & Lois Caughron lived in a small caretaker's cabin
near Lawson's cabin on the Loop Road in Cades Cove.
(Courtesy, National Park Service)

They lived without electricity or running water, although Kermit ran a
pipe from a spring higher up on the mountain down to the back porch of
the cabin. Kermit was a familiar sight to visitors in his overalls and floppy
hat, one foot propped on the rail fence at the front of the property, chatting
with visitors as they came by. Born in Cades Cove, he lived all but three of
his 87 years there. At one time, he kept bees and sold honey to the tourists
using an honor system, or a box where they could leave money in
exchange for a jar of honey. It's said he sometimes hid nearby to see if
people really left money in the box. Kermit's buried in Grandview
Cemetery on Tuckaleechee Pike in Maryville. His wife, Lois Shuler, lives
in Maryville, Tenn.

In Cataloochee, the last leaseholder to leave the Park was Lush Caldwell
(Flaugh, 2000). He leased land along Messer Fork before 1937 and leased

other tracts after that. He left the valley in 1968 when the leases became limited to the production of hay. That requirement continued into the 1980s.

Turkey George Palmer and Steve Woody stayed in Cataloochee until their deaths in 1939 and 1943, respectively. Several others stayed until 1945. The lease terms "restricted the cutting of timber and hunting; outlawed the manufacture, sale or possession of illegal liquor; required the leaseholders to fight fires and to enforce Park regulations; prohibited free ranging livestock as well as limiting the number and type of animals allowed and some fields were removed from using for any production" (Flaugh, 2000). As a result, most residents had no means to support themselves. By 1940, only 11 farms with 66 people in 16 families were left in the township of Cataloochee.

And so, most people eventually left their mountain homes. Some buildings were left in Cades Cove and Cataloochee, but in other areas the buildings were sold for scrap or burned (Van West, 1998).

The Great Smoky Mountains National Park was a success, at least in terms of popularity with the public. People seemed hungry for a chance to be in a natural, at least what seemed to be a wilderness setting, even if it was only to drive through it. Today, the number of visitors each year generally totals about nine million.

8 <u>Managing the Park</u>

The beauty of the Smoky Mountains and the perception of the region as an untamed wilderness prompted the idea of creating a national Park in order to preserve and protect such a wonderful natural environment almost in the middle of the country and within a day's drive of most of the large population centers of the eastern U.S. The idea that it had served as home to settlers and American Indians alike for hundreds of years received little attention.

As a result, the main thrust of planning for the Park followed the "assumption that the Park was to be a natural Park . . . " with the primary objective the protection of the natural environment." Evidence of human habitation in the Smokies was seen as a threat to the natural setting, especially evidence of recent human activity such as white-washed clapboard houses instead of log cabins. Such evidence didn't fit in with the idea of a pioneer settlement in an untamed wilderness.

However, there were those in the National Park Service (NPS) who recognized the contribution made to the area by the different groups of people who had been a part of the region. Three individuals in particular who worked for NPS played pivotal roles in seeing the value of preserving the human history and culture of the region: Hiram C. Wilburn, historian; Arthur Stupka, Park naturalist, and Charles P. Grossman, architect. Later, other individuals within the Park service including many Park rangers, archaeologists and historians helped nurture and push this idea forward. Without their insistance on the importance of finding and preserving cultural artifacts, the Great Smoky Mountains would have become a natural Park. The rich historical and cultural resources within the area of the Park would have been lost for all time.

As early as 1932, Park management began to realize the importance of the unique culture of the area. In the end, though, they decided to focus mainly on pioneer culture within the Park rather than any move toward modernization that had been made by individuals who'd lived in the Park in the late 1800s and early 1900s. Much of the more modern buildings had probably already been destroyed or sold by this time. Fortunately, many log structures didn't share this end. And so, they kept the best examples of pioneer log construction and began to preserve them. The few remaining frame structures in the Park include the Becky Cable house in Cades Cove, the buildings in Cataloochee and the Oconoluftee Baptist Church. They were allowed to remain.

The Historic Sites Act of 1935 supported the Park service's role in preserving historic structures, sites and objects for the benefit of the public. It also required that historic properties be surveyed in light of their historic worth (Flaugh, 2000). The same year, NPS architect Charles S. Grossman, along with Hiram C. Wilburn and Willis King, a CCC naturalist technician, conducted a building survey of the Park. The survey included taking photographs of every structure in the Park at that time. Another survey was conducted in Cataloochee in 1937. One of the reasons for the second survey was to determine which vacant buildings could be removed or destroyed. Such structures came under the heading of fire hazards and administrative problems for some within the Park service. The solution to the problem was removal or destruction.

This wasn't the first time homes and buildings in the Smokies had been destroyed by the government. It also happened in areas of North Carolina bought by TVA to build Fontana Dam. The buildings were torn down, then torched. Some watched their homes burn as they crossed the Tuskesegee River by boat.

Messer Applehouse, built by Will Messer, Cataloochee, moved to Oconoluftee Pioneer Farm. Originally, it was partially underground to insulate it from the summer heat and winter cold. *(Courtesy, www.wikipedia.org)*

Those who conducted the building survey of the Park structures in 1937 produced a report outlining a long-term program to preserve the mountain culture of the Park and a report on the human history of the area. Wilburn, Grossman, and Stupka prepared the report that presented a "cultural pattern of unique characteristics and historical importance." They proposed using cultural museums in which visitors could observe people living as they had lived during pioneer times. Although the idea of asking remaining Park residents to "play the role" of pioneer settlers in the Park proved unworkable, the Pioneer Farm at Oconaluftee and the Sugarlands Visitors Center are examples of the kinds of cultural exhibits suggested in their report.

Several buildings were moved from one area to another in order to form cultural exhibits such as the Pioneer Farmstead at Oconaluftee. One reason for moving structures from Cataloochee to Oconaluftee was that the Park Service decided to focus on areas that were accessible. Before WW II, the Civilian Conservation Corps played a major role in both maintenance and obliteration of buildings, as well as cemetery cleanup and road and trail reconstruction. Once the U.S. entered the war, however, the CCC camps closed, and the number of employees and funding fell away, a major blow to the Park Service.

9 Future of the Park

Great Smoky Mountains National Park can be considered a tremendous success, in terms of being the most visited National Park according to a 2010 National Park survey. That year GSMNP was the most visited park in the country with nine million visitors, more than half as many experienced in Yellowstone National Park. In addition, the survey shows visitors spent more than an estimated $818 million in gateway communities located around the boundaries of the Park. Because of this, the study estimates that 11,367 jobs in the area were supported by the spending of Park visitors (Stynes, 2010).

If number of visitors and money spent assures the future of GSMNP, this Park will enjoy a long and fruitful life. However, with all the success in attracting visitors to the Park, come problems. High traffic volume through areas such as Cades Cove, which receives about one-fourth the total number of visits as the Park itself, taxes the limits of the facilities there and sometimes create "bear jams" or, more often, "deer jams" as people stop their cars to view or photograph a bear or deer spotted along the way. Sometimes, thousands of dollars worth of camera equipment zero in on one small fawn nibbling at a spot of grass.

This, coupled with resistance by area residents to allowing modes of transportation into the Park that restrict their access, has caused Park personnel to create more pull off areas along the 11-mile loop road in Cades Cove, and posted signs to instruct motorists to pull over to allow others to move through the area. Bathroom facilities built in the 1960s are available only at the beginning of the loop road and at the mid-point of the loop and need upgrading.

NPS personnel are constantly looking for ways to raise funds to maintain and improve road and facility projects. Oconoluftee Visitor Center in North Carolina is a prime example of how this works. The updated visitors center facility in Oconoluftee, North Carolina, was unveiled in April of 2011. The new Center is a 6,300-square foot building with exhibits about the long history of the Parkland, from prehistoric times to the 20th century, and a store. Personnel offer information and orientation to visitors.

The new Oconoluftee Visitors Center.
(Courtesy, National Park Service)

Designed as a model of energy efficiency, this building has geothermal wells, solar tube lighting, rain water collectors and used recycled construction materials extensively. It was funded by donations from organizations that included Great Smoky Mountains Association (GSMA) and Friends of the Smokies. The Blue Ridge National Heritage Area provided a $20,000 grant to the Friends in support of creating interpretive exhibits within the museum. The project came to $3 million.

There were no public funds used for this project. Most likely, this will be typical of the sources looked to as aspects of GSMNP continue to need support and improvement.

Some cynics may suggest the popularity of GSMNP is, at least in part, due to the fact that this Park is the only one where no fees are charged for admission. That may well be the case for some, even many, folks. But the attractions that bring visitors into the region again and again seem to be the magnificent views of the mountains and the valley floor, a chance to see animals such as deer and bear in the wild and to see homes, churches and cemeteries of those who made the Smokies their homes in the late 1800s and early 1900s. Nostalgia for a perceived simpler life sometimes steals over visitors and brings them back.

Boys on Bote Mountain Trail with rolls of camping equipment in early days of Park. (*Courtesy, National Park Service*)

In addition to such cultural and historic draws, approximately 900 trails attract hikers who want to view vistas from Gregory Balds, Chimney Tops,

Appalachian Trail or LeConte Lodge. Birdwatchers have ample chances to look for birds in all types of habitats in the Smokies. Waterfalls and rivers offer scenic beauty and enable some to experience fishing or spotting an otter frolicking in a tranquil setting. Rustic camping sites are available for tents and sometimes RVs. Experiments, too, in bringing back animal species that were wiped out during the mid-1800s, such as elk, otter and barn owls, have proven to be successful.

Part of the Elk herd at Cataloochee grazing in an open field.
(Courtesy, Kathleen Puckett)

That likely means more species will be given a chance to come back, too. Frogs, toads and salamanders are already in abundant supply in the Smokies and, in fact, the Smokies are known as the "Salamander Capital of the World."

Bears are another species doing well in the Park, and, in 2012, scientists estimated that 1,500 black bears live in the Smokies, though that number changes from time to time, depending on availability of food sources. This estimate means there are about two bears per mile.

GSMNP has 384 miles of road, mostly paved, offering auto tours with panoramic views, mountain streams, historic buildings, mature hardwoods. *(Courtesy, Federal Highway Administration).*

The vision of those who first aspired to create a National Park in the Smoky Mountains seems to have come into being. Their goal of creating and maintaining the beauty of the place and preserving it for the enjoyment of all who visit looked incompatible. Somehow, though, NPS personnel seem to have been able to have some success in accomplishing both goals, at least for now.

The future of the Park depends on the ability of Park personnel to continue to focus on ways to accomplish both goals. As in its beginnings, when GSMNP became a reality through donations of pennies from schoolchildren and millions from individuals, so, too, as the Park moves into the future, much depends on that same kind of grassroots interest and support.

ABOUT THE AUTHOR

Dr. Gail Palmer has deep roots in East Tennessee and the Smoky Mountains. Her maternal grandparents, John Marion Sparks and Elizabeth Jane Shuler, both lived in Cades Cove. John was born there, while Elizabeth came from just over the mountain in Dry Valley, Tenn.

Palmer's feeling of connection to Cades Cove and the Smokies strengthened over time and fueled her curiosity about the mountains and the people who lived there. When she finished her degrees (undergraduate, masters and doctorate) at the University of Tennessee, Knoxville, she knew she could use what she had learned to find out even more about her ancestors and the region, and be able to share that with others.

Born in Maryville, Tenn., she attended schools in Dunedin and Clearwater, Fla., when her family moved there and where her parents (James and Mary Palmer) operated a small furniture store. She worked in various editorial and writing positions in Florida and New York. After moving to Knoxville, she worked in the office of the School of Journalism and finished a bachelor of science and masters in journalism. She served as the first adviser in the College's Advising Center and was eventually appointed director of the Center. She also served as an adjunct instructor in journalism and taught basic news writing.

Palmer began gathering material for a book on the Smokies soon after finishing her Ph.D. in 1994. She completed this work in 2006. Great Smoky Mountains Association is scheduled to publish it. Other work has appeared in national and local publications.

In 2009, she wrote and produced a DVD, "Sacred Places of the Smokies," featuring stories about individuals who lived in the Smokies before Great Smoky Mountains National Park was created. Then, in 2010, she wrote and produced a second DVD, "When Mama Was the Doctor: Medicine Women of the Smokies." Both DVDs are available at GRSM Visitors Centers, at venues in Maryville, Knoxville and Townsend, as well as www.amazon.com.

This is the first in a series of books she will publish about Great Smoky Mountains National Park and its people. Some of the topics may include *Smoky Mountain Romance*, *Smoky Mountain Murder & Mayhem*, *Smoky Mountain Curious Casket Tales*. Some stories are funny, some are sad, but all open a window into the world of the lives of these people, their character and how they viewed themselves and their world.

Other books in this series will feature stories about individuals who settled in the mountains, bringing their own stamp of originality, unique ways of thinking and creating families and lifetimes among these hills. The series will be available as eBooks and as paperback books on Amazon.com.

For more information about the following topics, go to www.gsmnp.org :

Air Quality,

All Taxa Biodiversity Inventory

Cades Cove Transportation and Development Planning,

Cell Towers

Elk Project

Elkmont Historic District

Foothills Parkway

Forest Insect and Disease

Hemlock Woolly Adelgid

North Shore Road

North Shore Road - Record of Decision

North Shore Road - 2010 Settlement Agreement

Tremont Facility Planning

Wild Hogs

BIBLIOGRAPHY

Adams, Inez and Earl. Personal interview, 2011.

Blackmun, Ora. <u>Western North Carolina, Its mountains and its people to 1880</u>. Appalachian Consortium Press, Boone, N.C. 1977.

Brewer, Alberta and Carson. <u>Valley So Wild: A Folk History</u>. East Tennessee Historical Society, Knoxville, Tenn. 1975.

Brown, Fred. <u>Knoxville's Legacy to Smokies: City's money, mayor, residents paved way for Great Smoky Mountains National Park</u>, Knoxville News-Sentinel, January 25, 2009.

Brown, Margaret Lynn. *The Wild East: A biography of the Great Smoky Mountains*. University Press of Florida, Orlando. 2000.

Burns, Inez P. <u>History of Blount County, Tennessee, From War Trail to Landing Strip, 1795-1955</u>. Nashville, 1973.

Bush, Florence Cope. <u>Dorie: Woman of the Mountains</u>. University of Tennessee Press, 1992.

Campbell, Carlos S. *Birth of a National Park in the Great Smoky Mountains*. The University of Tennessee Press. 1969.

Dykeman, Wilma. Tennessee: A Bicentennial History. W. W. Norton & Co., Inc., NY, 1975.

Dunn, Durwood. *Cades Cove: The Life and Death of A Southern Appalachian Community, 1818-1937*. The University of Tennessee Press. 1988.

Flaugh, Diane L. Cataloochee Historic District: Cultural Landscape Report, GSMNP, Jan. 2000, Draft.

Givens, Peter Shelburne. Master's Thesis: North Carolina, Western Carolina University, Cullowhee. 1978.

Groce, W. Todd. *Mountain Rebels: East Tennessee Confederates and the Civil War, 1860–1870*. UT Press, 1992.

Schmidt, Ronald G. & William S. Hooks. *Whistle Over the Mountain*. Ohio: Graphicom Press, 1994.

Shields, A. Randolph. The Cades Cove Story. Gatlinburg, Tenn., 1977.

Stynes, Daniel. *Economic Benefits to Local Communities from National Park Visitation and Payroll, 2010.* Michigan State University.

Trout, Ed. "Cades Cove Auto Tour," Great Smoky Mountains Natural History Association with National Park Service, 1976.

Van West, Carroll. *Tennessee History: The Land, the People and the Culture. 1998.*

Other works by Dr. Palmer

Books: Smoky Mountain Tales, Vol. 1: Feuds, Murder & Mayhem
DVDs: *Sacred Places of the Smokies; When Mama Was the Doctor: Medicine Women of the Smokies*

Works in progress

Smoky Mountain Tales Series
Vol. 2, More Feuds, Murder & Mayhem

Dr. Gail Palmer
Smoky Mountain Publishers
P.O. Box 684
Alcoa, TN 37701
lpalmer@utk.edu
865-724-4959

www.ingramcontent.com/pod-product-compliance
Lightning Source LLC
Chambersburg PA
CBHW051235090426
42740CB00001B/31